EARTH'S PRECIOUS WATER

HOW WATER SHAPES THE EARTH

by Blaine Wiseman

LIGHTBOX

Go to **www.openlightbox.com**, and enter this book's unique code.

ACCESS CODE

LBXR2366

Lightbox is an all-inclusive digital solution for the teaching and learning of curriculum topics in an original, groundbreaking way. Lightbox is based on National Curriculum Standards.

STANDARD FEATURES OF LIGHTBOX

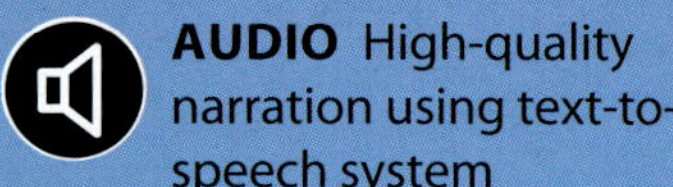

AUDIO High-quality narration using text-to-speech system

ACTIVITIES Printable PDFs that can be emailed and graded

SLIDESHOWS Pictorial overviews of key concepts

VIDEOS Embedded high-definition video clips

WEBLINKS Curated links to external, child-safe resources

TRANSPARENCIES Step-by-step layering of maps, diagrams, charts, and timelines

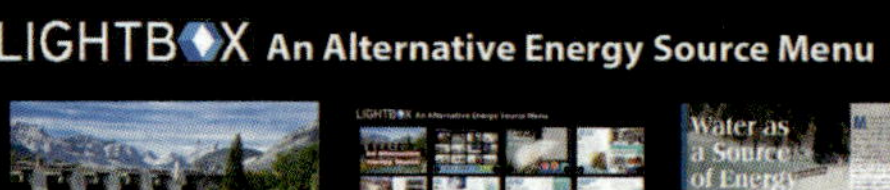

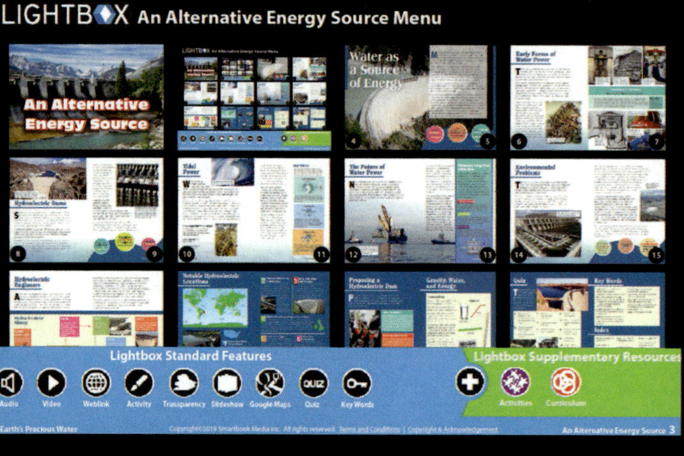

INTERACTIVE MAPS Interactive maps and aerial satellite imagery

QUIZZES Ten multiple choice questions that are automatically graded and emailed for teacher assessment

KEY WORDS Matching key concepts to their definitions

Contents

Water Cycle

Water is a building block for all life on Earth. It helps keep people healthy and clean. It plays an important role in growing and cooking the food that feeds us. It is essential to growing plants, which create the air we breathe. Water has the power to create and maintain life all over the world. It also has the power to influence how life is lived. Not only does life on Earth depend on water, but the planet itself is shaped by the power of water.

Earth is made of rocks, but it is mostly covered by water. In scientific terms, the rocks that make up Earth are known as the lithosphere, while Earth's water makes up the hydrosphere. Oceans, lakes, rivers, streams, ponds, **glaciers**, and **ice caps** hold the water that can be seen on Earth's surface. There is also much more water that is hidden from view. This includes **aquifers** underground and moisture in the soil. There is also a large amount of water floating in the air, or the atmosphere. Finally, water can be found in all of Earth's lifeforms, which make up the biosphere.

Earth's four spheres interact with each other, and water moves between them. This is known as the water cycle. All of the water on Earth is part of this cycle. Water in the atmosphere falls back to the ground as rain. From there, it can soak into the soil or flow into an ocean, river, lake, or aquifer. It may end up relieving the thirst of an animal. Eventually, it will **evaporate**, returning to the air as vapor. This cycle of moving water has a major effect on Earth and all its lifeforms.

About **71 percent of Earth** is covered in water.

More than **96 percent** of Earth's water is salt water.

More than **68 percent** of Earth's fresh water is **frozen in glaciers and ice caps**.

Erosion

The movement of water is constantly changing Earth. It is easy to see examples of this by looking at waves on a beach or at rainwater flowing through a garden. The moving grains of sand or the channels created in the dirt are examples of **erosion**. Ice, water, and wind are the three natural forces that cause erosion. Any time one of these forces moves or changes a rock, a clump of soil, or a grain of sand, erosion is happening. It may seem like erosion makes small changes, but over long periods of time, it has a major impact on Earth's surface.

As the ice from a glacier on a mountaintop melts, it turns to water and runs downhill, creating a small channel in the dirt. When this small amount of water reaches a cliff, it will drip down to the bottom. This dripping wears away at the rocks below the cliff, creating a small divot where the water gathers. Over time, more and more water will melt from the glacier and enter the channel, making it deeper and wider. Eventually, the channel may become a stream or a river. The water dripping from the cliff may become a waterfall, and the small divot could turn into a lake.

Moving water is one of the most powerful forces on Earth. It has the strength to carve away even the strongest rock. Many of the world's major **geographic features**, including lakes, rivers, canyons, valleys, and caves, were created by the forces of erosion.

EROSION EXAMPLES

Type	Source
Coastal Cliff	Wave
Valley	River
Topsoil Loss	Wind
Glacial Erratics	Moving Glaciers
Landslide	Gravity

The Grand Canyon is 277 miles (446 kilometers) long and 18 miles (29 km) wide at its widest point.

Rocks as old as 2 billion years have been discovered at the bottom of the Grand Canyon.

People have lived in the Grand Canyon for at least 900 years. The first known inhabitants were the Pueblo Peoples.

The Grand Canyon

When: About 6 million years ago | **Where:** Grand Canyon National Park, Arizona

The Grand Canyon is one of the world's most obvious and spectacular examples of erosion. Over millions of years, water from the Colorado River has worn away the ground, creating the canyon. More than five million people visit the canyon every year to take pictures, hike, and witness the power of erosion. Even after millions of years, the effects of erosion are still changing the Grand Canyon every day.

DISCUSSION
What benefits can erosion have for people? Think about ways people have benefitted from living in or near the Grand Canyon.

Every year, the Grand Canyon experiences flooding. This helps to move sand and rocks through the canyon.

Flooding the canyon helps maintain an environment where fish, including the humpback chub, can survive. This endangered species relies on high water conditions for breeding and feeding.

The Grand Canyon is more than a mile (1.6 km) deep.

About 90 percent of the ocean moves with deep water currents called the global conveyor belt. It helps algae and seaweed to grow by distributing nutrients and carbon dioxide throughout the oceans.

Oceans and Lakes

Scientists identify five different oceans, but the Pacific, Atlantic, Indian, Southern, and Arctic Oceans are actually all connected. Lakes are also connected to the oceans, either by the water cycle or by **watersheds**. Lakes can vary in size, but they are much smaller than oceans, and are mostly surrounded by land. While there are many differences between oceans and lakes, they both have the power to shape the land.

Currents are the movement of water in a certain direction. These can occur at or near the surface of the water, or deep below. They can be slow-moving or fast-moving, depending on the forces behind them. Some surface currents are powered by wind, which also causes waves. The most powerful and fastest-moving currents are tidal currents. These are caused by gravitational pull from the Sun and Moon. As Earth rotates, the force of gravity from the Sun and Moon causes water on Earth to move in certain ways.

This is what causes tides to rise and fall each day. Gravitational pull creates tides that scientists can observe and predict. This helps them understand when and where water levels will rise and fall.

About 100 billion tons (91 billion metric tons) of water flow in and out of the Bay of Fundy with each tide. This happens every 12 hours and 26 minutes.

Strong winds can cause powerful waves to travel across the surface of water and crash into the shore. In Lake Huron, scientists have observed an effect called shoreline erosion, which has both negative and positive impacts on the people who live by the lake. Shoreline erosion happens when waves drag sand from the shore back into the water. Currents then carry the sand through the water and deposit it somewhere else. This can take land away from one area, leaving homes or properties dangerously close to the water. However, the sand that is deposited elsewhere can build beaches, creating a new environment there.

Lake Baikal, in Russia, is the world's **deepest lake**.

About **one fifth** of the **world's freshwater** is in Lake Baikal.

Lake Baikal formed between **20 and 25 million** years ago.

Scientists estimate that one inch of rain falling over a 1 square-mile (1.6 sq. km) area is equal to about 17.4 million gallons (65.9 million liters) of water.

Water and Weather

Weather is the temperature, moisture, wind, and pressure people feel in a certain area over a short period of time. This can be minutes, hours, or days. When people check the weather, they are wondering what the conditions are like at that moment in their area. Scientists who study the weather can use the water in and around that area to understand how the weather will change.

The relationship between weather and water is obvious when it rains, but even hot, dry, sunny weather moves water. When people look up in the sky and see clouds, they are looking at water. Clouds are water vapor that has evaporated from oceans, lakes, and other water sources, and entered the atmosphere. Water vapor gathers together to form clouds, which are a sign of changing weather. Eventually, the vapor in a cloud will turn back into liquid water and fall back to Earth as rain, sleet, snow, or hail. Water that falls from the sky is known as precipitation.

Cherrapunji, India

The town of Cherrapunji, India, is known for its heavy rains. It holds the record for the heaviest rainfall in a two day period. These rains fell as part of a monsoon, which is a period of heavy rainfall that occurs each year in areas of Asia. Cherrapunji also holds the record for the most rain in a single year.

Most Rainfall in a Single Year
When: August 1860 to July 1861
Amount: 86.8 feet (26 m)

Heaviest Rainfall in a Two-Day Period
Year: 1995
Amount of Rain: 98 inches (2.5 m)

When precipitation falls back to Earth, it helps plants grow and can give people and animals water to drink. As it strikes the ground and flows across it, precipitation also causes erosion. Snow and ice can cause especially large changes to the ground, but these changes may take longer to happen. Glaciers create the most obvious examples of such changes, taking years, centuries, or even millennia to carve a channel as they melt.

Glaciers can create large U-shaped valleys as they melt. Glacier National Park in Montana was formed by large glaciers that moved rock and soil as they crossed the land.

Climate and Water

Climate is related to weather but is used to describe the general weather patterns of an area over a longer period of time. There are six major types of climate in the world. They are dependent on the type and amount of water in their weather systems. Polar climates are cold and dry. Tundra climates are also cold, but wetter than polar climates. Arid climates are hot and dry. Temperate climates have cold winters and mild summers. Mediterranean climates have hot, dry summers and mild winters. Tropical climates are hot and wet all year.

The plants, animals, and people of an area are adapted to surviving in the climatic conditions of that area. When climate patterns change, it can create major problems. If a temperate area does not receive enough rain, crops may not grow, causing a drought. If too much rain falls, it can cause flooding. Unusually warm weather in polar climates causes ice to melt. Too much melting ice can cause sea levels and temperatures to rise. This may flood coastal areas. Warming sea water changes weather patterns, currents, and animals' migration patterns.

Greenland's polar ice sheet covers about 80 percent of the island's surface, and is currently melting at a rate of about 110 million Olympic-size swimming pools each year. If the entire ice sheet melted, global sea level would rise by about 24 feet (7.2 meters).

Tuvalu

Tuvalu is a country in the Indian Ocean. It is a series of tropical islands. During the last several decades, Tuvaluans have noticed their islands are shrinking as sea levels rise. This has caused many islanders to leave their country, fearing it will one day disappear completely. The president of Tuvalu has spoken to the United Nations, asking for help solving the issue. Tuvalu has even considered suing other countries for causing global warming and rising sea levels.

TUVALU BY THE NUMBERS

- Tuvalu only has 10 square miles (26 sq. km) of dry land, making it one of the smallest countries in the world.
- Tuvalu's highest elevation is only 15 feet (4.6 m) above sea level.
- Erosion caused Tuvalu's Tepuka Island to shrink by 22 percent since 1896.
- A type of microscopic lifeform called star sand makes up about 66 percent of the land on Tuvalu. When the creatures die, their shells turn into sand. Tuvaluans have begun cultivating star sand and placing it in coastal areas in order to grow their shorelines.
- Between 2005 and 2015, about 15 percent of Tuvalu's population left the country.
- Since 1993, the sea level around Tuvalu has risen 0.2 inches (5 millimeters) faster than the world's average.
- Since 1970, Tuvalu's total land area has actually grown by almost three percent. This is due to changing wave patterns bringing more sand to some of Tuvalu's 101 islands.

Building on the Coast

Living near a river, lake, or ocean can make it easy to gather water, to fish, or to travel. Leisure activities such as swimming, boating, surfing, fishing, and beach volleyball also attract people to beachfront living. However, despite these benefits, there are serious drawbacks to living near the water.

The first civilizations grew in fertile areas near the Euphrates and Tigris rivers in the Middle East. Powerful civilizations later grew in other areas of the world, such as the Hwang Ho River in China, and Lake Texcoco in Mexico. In order to live in these coastal areas, each society had to prepare for and manage erosion.

The city of Tenochtitlan was built on Lake Texcoco. To protect it from erosion, the Aztec peoples made levees, or raised banks, around the city.

Today, some beachfront property owners have built seawalls to block waves from reaching their property. While this protects their own land from erosion, it can send larger waves down the beach, making erosion worse for their neighbors. Areas along the Gulf of Mexico, such as Louisiana, Florida, Alabama, and Texas, have experienced serious erosion in the past few years. This is caused by a combination of factors including severe weather and industrial processes. Dams in the Mississippi River have reduced the amount of **sediment** reaching the gulf shores. Strong waves, driven by hurricane winds, have swamped coastal areas and washed away beaches.

Sometimes, construction vehicles move new sand toward the shoreline to rebuild eroded beaches. After large waves in Nags Head, North Carolina, new sand is often needed to fix the erosion.

In some places affected by these issues, people have begun building living shorelines. Planting specific types of marsh grasses in the sand helps create a natural barrier on the shore that is able to stand up to strong waves. Some communities even bring sand in by boat and dump it in coastal areas to replace what has been eroded away.

The **first known civilizations** began in Mesopotamia around **5,000 years** ago.

Tenochtitlán was located in **the middle** of **Lake Texcoco**.

Half of the city of New Orleans, Louisiana, is below sea level. The sea is held back by levees.

Climatologists

Weather scientists, called meteorologists, look at the current conditions of an area to predict how warm, wet, or windy it will be for the next few days. A scientist who studies long-term climates is called a climatologist. These highly trained specialists study how climates behave, change, and how they can affect the weather in the past, present, and future.

While people have studied climate since early history, it was not until the early 20th century that scientists began to truly understand it.

Climatology History

1895–1932

Norwegian scientist Vilhelm Bjerknes makes several important breakthroughs in the study of weather and climate. These include the circulation of heat and water in the atmosphere, along with new methods of predicting the weather.

1922

Lewis Fry Richardson, a British scientist, develops a method for predicting weather using math to observe currents in air and water. Richardson's method is still used today in the fields of meteorology and climatology.

1942

The University of Chicago creates the first Department of Meteorology. Researchers in the department develop the first global climate model, which views the entire world as a single, connected climate system.

The quality and ability of understanding climate improved drastically as computers became more powerful in the 1950s. Since then, equipment and processes have improved even more.

Climatologists can work for businesses, governments, universities, and **non-profit organizations**. They use equipment such as satellites, computers, and **barometers**. In order to become a climatologist, a person must have a passion for studying climate and weather, and they must do well in school. Science and math are especially important. Climatologists often start by studying meteorology before moving on to a Master's Degree in climatology, and then studying even more to earn a **doctorate**.

1963

Dr. J. Murray Mitchell, Jr. and his colleagues perform research showing that rising global temperatures are linked to human pollution.

1970

The U.S. government founds the National Oceanic and Atmospheric Administration (NOAA). This organization combines several scientific disciplines to help scientists better understand how climate is affected by the ocean and the atmosphere.

2018

The U.S. government creates the Challenges and Prizes for Climate Act of 2018. The program aims to challenge researchers and scientists to make breakthroughs that will help slow climate change. Successful competitors will be awarded prizes to help develop their new technologies, systems, and products.

Shaping the World

1 Buffalo, United States

In October 2006, the city of Buffalo was hit by one of the most severe **blizzards** in U.S. history, caused by climatic conditions called the Lake Effect. When cold, dry air passes over a large body of warm water, the air picks up heat and moisture. This rapid warming and moistening of the air causes precipitation, which then falls as snow. The 2006 storm dumped almost 23 inches (58 cm) of snow on Buffalo.

2 Bay of Fundy, Canada

The Bay of Fundy experiences the world's highest tide. Over the course of six hours twice every day, the water level in the bay raises by more than 50 feet (15 m). This is more than all of the water flowing through the world's freshwater rivers in the same time period. Rocks in the Bay of Fundy have eroded into unique formations from the constant powerful forces of the tides.

3 Pine Island Glacier, Antarctica

Antarctica's Pine Island Glacier is the fastest-melting glacier in the world. Between 1974 and 2007, melting sped up by 73 percent. In 2015, a chunk of ice measuring 224 square miles (580 sq. km) broke away from the glacier and fell into the sea. If the entire glacier melted, it would raise global sea levels by about 5.5 feet (1.7 m).

4 Okavango Delta, Botswana

The Okavango Delta is an area of wetlands and grasslands in Botswana that acts as an oasis in the middle of the Kalahari Desert. Each year, during the dry season, an average of 2.5 trillion gallons (9.5 trillion L) of water flows into Botswana's delta basin. When the waters arrive, so do millions of animals.

5 Sarawak Chamber, Malaysia

Sarawak Chamber is the largest known cavern in the world. It is part of a larger cave complex called Nasib Bagus. The caves were formed over thousands of years by water draining through the forest floor, creating an aquifer. The Sarawak Chamber measures 2,300 feet (700 m) long, 1,312 feet (400 m) at its widest point, and 230 feet (70 m) high. The chamber is so big, it could hold about 40 Boeing 747 airplanes.

6 Solomon Islands

The Solomon Islands are a country made up of more than 900 islands and **atolls**. In 2016, scientists reported that five of the country's islands had been washed away by rising sea levels and erosion, and that six more were in danger. In the Solomon Islands, levels are rising at a rate of more than twice the global average.

Changing Weather

Earth's climate has changed throughout history. Some places become warmer, receiving less snowfall than before. Other places see changes in the amount of rainfall during certain seasons. Research how climate and weather have changed in your area over the last few decades. Check online archives, the library, and talk to people who have lived in the area for a long time.

WHAT IS HAPPENING?

Chart the trends of your local climate and weather over time. Note average temperatures and precipitation levels. Look for differences between the start and end of your chart.

WHAT ARE THE EFFECTS?

How have changes in the local weather affected the area? Have changes in precipitation caused flooding or droughts? Have plants and animals been affected by the changes in weather?

WHAT CAN BE DONE?

What can people or governments in your area do to address these changes? Have any laws been passed to reduce pollution, emissions, or consumption? Can changes in behavior help fix the situation? Think about ways people can adapt to changing weather.

Simulate Erosion

Materials

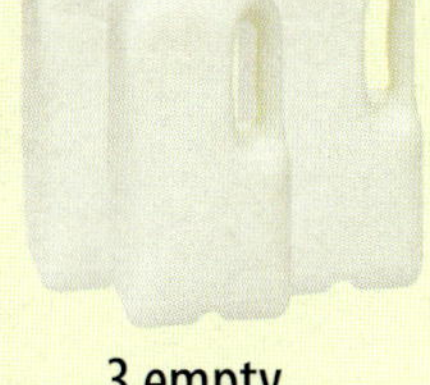

3 empty, plastic milk jugs

3 empty, clear plastic water bottles with caps on

Scissors

Grass seed or potted plants

Water

Measuring cup

Instructions

Step 1: Lay each milk jug on its side and cut an opening on the top side, leaving the spout intact. Cut the bottoms out of the water bottles and leave the caps on. Hang them from the spouts of the milk jugs.

Step 2: Take the caps off the milk jugs. Fill each milk jug with soil to a level just below the spout. In the first jug, plant your grass seed or potted plants. In the second jug, layer the top of the soil with the twigs, leaves, or wood chips. Leave the soil in the third jug bare.

Step 3: Lift the back end of the jugs slightly so the spouts point down. Water one of the jugs and watch the water flow through the soil and into the collector bottle. Repeat this process for each of the other jugs.

Step 4: Measure how much water was collected in each plastic bottle. Note the color of the runoff water, and how much sediment collected in each one.

Step 5: Discuss with your class the differences between each jug and the runoff it produced. Talk about the types of environments each jug simulated and where you have seen this type of soil before. Discuss ways people can treat soil responsibly to minimize erosion.

Quiz

Test your knowledge by answering these questions. All of the information can be found in the text you just read. The answers are provided below for easy reference.

1. Which of Earth's spheres is made up of the world's water?

2. What do people call the movement of dirt, sand, or rocks by water?

3. How many oceans are there?

4. What is the word for water that falls from the atmosphere back to Earth?

5. Which city was built on Lake Texcoco?

6. How many types of climate are there?

7. What is the name for the study of climate?

8. Which government agency studies the oceans, atmosphere, and climate?

9. What is the world's fastest-melting glacier?

10. What weather effect caused the Buffalo blizzard of 2006?

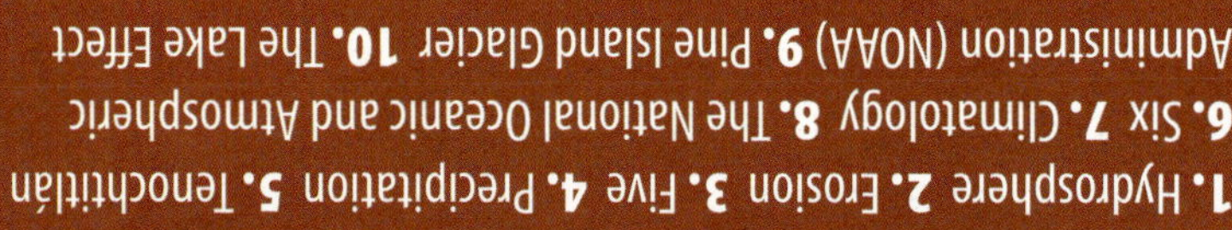

ANSWER KEY

1. Hydrosphere **2.** Erosion **3.** Five **4.** Precipitation **5.** Tenochtitlán **6.** Six **7.** Climatology **8.** The National Oceanic and Atmospheric Administration (NOAA) **9.** Pine Island Glacier **10.** The Lake Effect

Key Words

aquifers: underground chambers that holds water

atolls: ring-shaped islands or coral reefs

barometers: instruments that measure pressure in the atmosphere

blizzards: severe snow storms

doctorate: a certificate of education held by doctors

erosion: the wearing-away of a surface

evaporate: turn from liquid into vapor

geographic features: landforms

glaciers: slow-moving masses of ice

ice caps: large coverings of ice, usually at the poles of the planet

non-profit organizations: organizations that do not earn money

sediment: matter that settles in a liquid

watersheds: areas where water arrives or leaves an area

Index

LIGHTBOX

SUPPLEMENTARY RESOURCES

Click on the plus icon found in the bottom left corner of each spread to open additional teacher resources.

- Download and print the book's quizzes and activities
- Access curriculum correlations
- Explore additional web applications that enhance the Lightbox experience

LIGHTBOX DIGITAL TITLES

Packed full of integrated media

VIDEOS

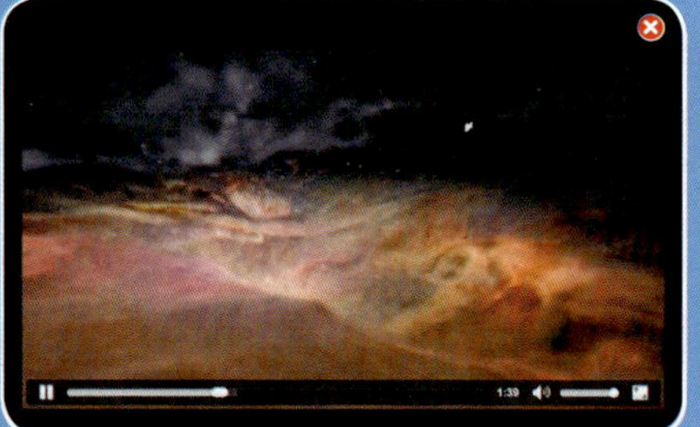

INTERACTIVE MAPS

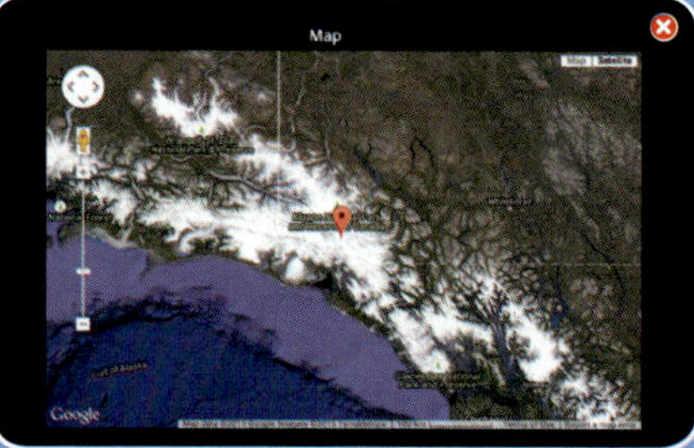

WEBLINKS

SLIDESHOWS

QUIZZES

OPTIMIZED FOR

- ✔ TABLETS
- ✔ WHITEBOARDS
- ✔ COMPUTERS
- ✔ AND MUCH MORE!

Published by Smartbook Media Inc.
350 5th Avenue, 59th Floor
New York, NY 10118
Website: www.openlightbox.com

Library of Congress Control Number: 2018944573

ISBN 978-1-5105-3885-6 (hardcover)
ISBN 978-1-5105-3886-3 (multi-user eBook)

Printed in Brainerd, Minnesota, United States
1 2 3 4 5 6 7 8 9 0 22 21 20 19 18

072018
120517

Project Coordinator John Willis
Art Director Terry Paulhus

Photo Credits
Every reasonable effort has been made to trace ownership and to obtain permission to reprint copyright material. The publisher would be pleased to have any errors or omissions brought to its attention so that they may be corrected in subsequent printings. The publisher acknowledges Alamy, Getty Images, iStock, Minden Pictures, Newscom, and Shutterstock as its primary image suppliers for this title.